A Darker Way

I Sally, Haf ac Alaw

A Darker Way

Grahame Davies

Seren is the book imprint of
Poetry Wales Press Ltd.
Suite 6, 4 Derwen Road, Bridgend,
Wales, CF31 1LH

www.serenbooks.com
Follow us on social media @SerenBooks

The right of Grahame Davies to be identified as
the author of this work has been asserted in accordance
with the Copyright, Designs and Patents Act, 1988.

ISBN: 978-1-78172-751-5
ebook: 978-1-78172-758-4

A CIP record for this title is available from the British Library.

The publisher acknowledges the financial assistance of the Books Council of Wales.

Cover painting: 'Pen y Fan at Dusk' by Jess Hinsley.

Contents

Scar

It was an open wound.
I treasured it, stigmatic
without sainthood,
weeping words, the grief
a price worth paying.
So I paid,
every few months,
for more than four decades,
a deal I never doubted:
poems for pain.

It's healing now.
That once-familiar ache
comes only rarely,
doesn't break the skin,
recedes before the mind can diagnose
what trouble this time tunnels to the light.
Peace makes no poems;
blessing brings no blood,
and calls no martyr to the marketplace.
Only, sometimes, for others,
if they ask,
the broken ones,
the ones who have no words,
but need them,
only those who'll never tell,
and never understand,
the sting will come.
And this is better now,
better by far: the wound
that has no words, the secret scar.

Farewell to poetry

They used to stack up,
waiting in the sky
a long perspective of receding lights
out of the blackness,
coming in to land.
Stare at the dark for long enough,
you'd find
a star detach itself and float to earth.
And always more to come.
But that was then.
The last one landed long ago,
the last
cargo delivered,
travellers dispersed.
Grass is encroaching on
the tarmac now. The runway
lights are off,
the tower's dark.
The gate unguarded.
Without knowing why,
I find this better:
silence after sound,
and solitude after society,
simply to walk out on the empty field,
feeling the wind across the open land,
expecting nothing from the empty sky.

Diaries

We say this is our now or never move:
the final chance to get the country house
while time enough remains to savour it.
Of course it's bigger than we need, but then
our lives seem bigger now. More memories,
more friends to welcome and more things to share.
While moving here, I found my diaries:
left in a drawer some thirty years ago:
no, more than that – I'm older than I thought.
The covers are as red as new-spilt blood.
The writing's recognisable as mine,
but cramped and urgent, filling every line
as though I thought that God would punish me
for wasting paper or for wasting time.
Which probably I did. Dear God, the purity –
it hurt my eyes to look at it. And vanity –
that I should think these inky agonies
would ever be of any interest.
The day I wrote them for has come, and I
could not care less about them now. He's dead,
the boy who biroed handed-down beliefs
as though for some divine, end-time exam.
And yet I do care. Not for what he thought –
deluded junk as dead as alchemy –
but what he felt: the sacrifice, the pain,
the opportunities he let go by,
the pleasures he forswore, and, even worse,
the pain he caused by perfect principle.
I want to speak to him: to tell him God
is not so cruel, so simple, or so pure.
My poor young self. I want to hold him close.
But I might just as well embrace a blade,
fire-forged and tempered and compassionless.
I am not angry with him, but with those
whose furnace faith turns men like that to steel.
It rusted in the end, much later on –
too late for many things. I put them back,
the diaries – today is not the time.
We have a house to furnish. It will come
the time to read them, maybe when we move
a final time in search of something small –
that vacant place awaits us, after all.

One human soul

One human soul. That's what the poster said
outside the wall of my new residence.
An ancient wall this, older than the house,
they say, and there's a man who lives nearby
can read its masonry like a book
and tell you where the stone came from, and when.
It's medieval, that's enough for me;
and listed, like the rest of the estate.
The poster looks like an advertisement,
tied to a lamppost with a piece of string,
the kind put up to find a missing cat,
'beloved family pet', that kind of thing.
Yet this one's seeking not to find, but sell.
A prank, it must be. Look at the address:
TheEvilOne, the @ sign, then dot com.
Some teenage goth. A guessing game. A dare.
I was a teenage goth, and would have sold
my soul to be what I have now become,
and have just realised it, much too late.
Maybe I did sell, not in one clear deal;
not in my own blood on a parchment page.
But that's not how it works, my black-clad friend,
my teenaged self. You sign, and never know.
You pay it in instalments, drop by drop,
and never know till it's too late to stop.

Speedway Eddie

Always, his head is bleeding:
every time he stumbles past you in the street,
reels in the road or slumps against a wall,
clutching the dull gold gleam of Special Brew,
or huddles in a doorway, left for dead.
His speedway jacket, garish once,
is grey with road grime.
He was fast, they said.
But then, that corner always was a bitch.
I'm not so sure. From what I've heard
he never was a racer, just a fan.
Maybe we need to think that tragedy
must be the only way to break a man.

Happy Larry's Funeral

We all knew Happy Larry. Or at least
we thought we did. He was that kind of man;
one of those characters, born middle aged,
that never stray five miles from where they're born,
 – their shortcomings, complete sufficiency,
their limitations, lifelong liberty –
who treat the High Street like their living room
and everyone they meet there like a friend.
Although, of course, we knew he had no friends,
or wife, or children, just acquaintances,
a village full. Old Larry never changed
his conversation, clothes or countenance –
One smile fits all. That's what they used to say –
and never aged. He never needed to.
Today I visited the place again,
a stranger in a suit, my family
just names on headstones now. It's been a while.
I heard the voices as I closed the gate
and took the gravel path between the yews.
The burial service. When you have to leave,
those are the words to leave to. Dignity.
The little group beside the open grave
are making their farewells: some locum priest,
no-one I know, the sexton with his spade
and one old lady, dabbing at her eyes.
She greets me as I pass. So sad, she says.
We were the only mourners that he had.
She's English. New to here, but not, I guess,
to sorrow, which makes siblings of us all.
They called him Happy Larry. No-one knew
his real name. But he always smiled at me.
I watched her as she set beside the cross
a bunch of garage flowers in cellophane
and went her way. It's been a while,
a long while, Larry, whom I never knew.
I've been away from home so many years
making a living, making money, making what
I told myself would be a better world,
but could not make, myself, that simple thing,
a place for Larry to be happy in.

Prayer

I thank you, Lord, that I was tested young.
The green tree bends when rainstorms come,
and springs back stronger.
And nothing the rain or wind or sun can bring,
and neither the fear of axe or lightning
can make it less than all that it should be.
Don't ask me now for what you asked me then.
Then, when I knew you less, I trusted more.
And others, seeing, trusted you in me,
and you did not betray them.
Nor did I.
They can still trust me.
Largely.
They still can.
But do not put me to the test.
I could not do it now.
I could not hold the psalm against the storm.
I know too much.
The worm has done what lightning could not do:
wisdom has made me weak, discretion brought decay,
and I would break: that is my truth now.
Conceal the rotten heartwood from the light.
Let earth take me in due season, unobserved.
And let that time I stood, let that time be
all you remember, when you remember me.

Solstice

I am sad now the solstice has gone.
I wanted to go deeper, darker, inward all the time.
There is some secret, maybe, hidden in the night.
It may be understanding.
It may be death.
It is, whatever it may be, my own,
and all the more so the further from the day.
But we have veered away again,
steering a course for the light.
I go with it.
For now.

Centenary Square, Birmingham

I thought at first it was a protest march,
the screechy, urgent, amplified address
echoing outside the public library,
or maybe some old street evangelist,
driven by conscience, self-conceit, or both
to pitch his sermons to the public square.
Except there were no crowds there to convert,
and no-one, in that wet November wind
to listen to those hissing solipsisms.
But still the disembodied voice went on,
sounding as though it issued from the earth.

      Because, I found, it did: a circled space
let down beneath the centre of the square,
where passers-by can look down from the rail
at those below, and listen – if they dare.
A writers' group are queueing for the mic,
to read, in turn, to nobody at all.

      It seemed, I thought, a special ring of Hell,
reserved, perhaps, for those who'd used their wit
to hurt, not heal, and sentenced for all time,
to bawl banalities through broken mics
with no-one there to hear, no audience,
except unsympathetic passers-by
to witness that they had no audience.
They read to empty air and empty walls,
tenacious and intense, and talentless,
All of them. Dreadful. Unredeemable.

      Their sole, unseen observer, I look round
for someone who can share the spectacle.
No experts needed: anyone will do.

      Two teenage girls have joined me at the rail,
hijabed and poppied both, and curious.
We watch the latest reader take her turn,

clutching her pages wrapped in polythene
and shaking with conviction, or the cold
I look towards the girls as if to ask
what do they think? As if I didn't know.
They know as well as I, but look away,
and whoop and clap, for kindness, and walk on,
reproaching me by what they did not say.
And I walk on as well, a darker way.

Travellers

Yes, we were nervous when they came, at first.
I won't deny it. All the things you hear –
the papers, that TV show – honestly,
the things that people say – you'd not believe.
So yes, there was apprehension, that's for sure.
But now, well, it's all worked out as you see.
          We didn't have the numbers any more:
the roof leaked and the boiler wouldn't work.
And people now – they just don't want to come.
And I don't blame them. So we struggled on.
And struggle it was too.
                          And then they came.
So many kids they didn't have the space
for play, for lessons, just for hanging out.
And so we did the deal.
                        They fixed the roof,
in no time, and the boiler and the floor.
And, yes, they did those murals. You can tell?
No, not to everybody's taste, but then,
neither was flaking whitewash, come to that.
Give me this noise and colour any day,
even the mess: it doesn't bother me.
At least, not any more. The mess is life.
And yes, they come to some of our events
and we to some of theirs. Ours. Theirs.
I'm not sure these things matter now. Ours. Ours.

Mission

It used to be a mission hall, I guess,
when running missions was the thing to do
back in the day – helping the worthy poor,
the orphans, fallen women – what you will,
and giving them what you thought they should want:
seeing your virtue in their gratitude.
A different age. The church closed long ago,
although it was a theatre for a while.
That didn't last. Nobody comes here now.
But it's still sound, the building, all the same.
Good for a few years yet: a varnished stage,
all clutter cleared away, an empty space,
filled with the evening sun,
swept clean and ready to be used again,
not minding if it's for a mission now,
or for a play, a meeting, anything.
Or nothing. That would suit it just as well.
The door is closed, not locked. The sign is new,
facing the high street: Empty Hall for Hire.

Familiar

I walked her home.
We took the long way round
just to prolong the time out of the house.
We'd known each other nearly forty years
and still I'm happy just to follow her.
We passed the dealership.
She touched the fence.
Short cut? she asked me.
If you want, I said.
Knowing she could not mean it.
Diwedd mawr...
– not in the heels that she was wearing now.
But still I would have done it if she'd said.
She turned away a few steps.
And was gone,
shoes in her hand, a county athlete,
a plastic medal winner with the Urdd,
I ran off after her.
Heads turned.
She didn't care,
cornering the terraces like a hare.
I knew where she was heading.
Out of breath,
I found her setting out a glass for me.
The usual?
I don't have a usual.
But took it from her gladly just the same.
But then, perhaps I do.
This race.
This game.

Survivor

What had he done to her? Her eyes
were black. The bruising spread
across them like a mask.
The interviewer's questioning was slow,
professional, the dressing
of a wound.
She'd never cried.
She left that all to him,
repenting and returning like the tide.
What did the church do when she let them know?
The closed eyes were the answer.
And her friends?
Behind her, out of focus,
altar plate. They polished that.
And yet she still believed?
Of course she did.
The eyes were open now,
brittle as stained glass
and as beautiful.
The tears came too
– to me –
I welcomed them,
and hoped that my companion saw them too,
and would, like me, accept my alibi.
knowing you can't be cruel
if you can cry.

Escape

One day I'll just keep walking,
and keep that long-held promise to myself,
like I was free again, like I was young,
running away from home.
One day I'll just keep walking,
past where familiar becomes strange. And on.
Shouts from the playground, traffic on the road,
wind through the hedgerows. On.
No one to miss me. No one to ask why.
        That would be freedom: never to be known,
and so, never forgotten, never recalled.
Never regretting. Never going back.
        And live how? Is that the question?
Right now I'd sooner ask: live why?
Because truth never seeks tranquillity;
it pays no house calls – a lifetime tells me that.
And so, one day, I'll just keep walking,
never expecting to arrive,
taking no map, no timepiece and no name.
One day I'll just keep walking from this town,
and leave as unencumbered as I came.

Colleague

All credit to her, she was quite an act.
She dazzled clients, left them wanting more,
Our bosses too: they couldn't get enough.
Outsiders loved her; colleagues – not so much.
the high-neck blouse, the handbag dog, the Merc,
the smile that saw them as they saw themselves,
approved, admired, and always in command.
She lied to people, was the simple fact,
and yet they seemed to love her all the same.

    It couldn't last, of course; it never could;
everyone saw it coming except her.
We held the door for justice when it came,
and, when she left, we tried hard not to stare,
and tried, a little, not to show we knew
the Queen of Parties had no leaving do.

    And that was months ago. I kept no count.
The irreplaceable is soon replaced,
and filed away with last year's promises.
I didn't think of her, perhaps from fear
that thought should somehow summon her again,
I guessed what she'd be doing, somewhere else.
People like that, they just keep moving on:
the act's the same, only the theatres change.

    Last night, late home and nothing in the fridge,
I thought I'd phone out for a takeaway.
And when the doorbell went, I took a pound
to give the courier – it was a filthy night.
She thanked me. I looked up. I knew the voice,
and knew the smile above the high-neck top.

    It pays the bills, she said. And keeps me fit
– She wasn't joking. She looked fabulous. –
Fitter than you'll be if you eat all that.
I see it keeps you honest too, I said.
I hope it will, she said. I hope it will.
Her mobile went. Another run. Goodbye.

    The rain was heavier now. I went inside,
and as I closed the door I could have wept,
and not with pity for her, but with pride.

Message

There is no future life. That's what it said.
A study showed – all those Near Death reports
are fallacies, are flawed, are fantasy.
A sober message for a children's book,
but necessary maybe. It was clear,
however much we might wish otherwise
there was no room for wishful thinking here.
The washed-out picture on the facing page
seemed to show fashions from decades ago.
When was this book produced? When I was young.
The early nighteen eighties. Yesterday.
Under the sun, they say, there's nothing new.
They're right: the sunlight bleaches everything,
turns newness to nostalgia, shade by shade,
and, page by page, fades hope to memory.
I put the book back on the bargain shelf
and step outside again into the sun.
I didn't need that message. We all know.
Believer, unbeliever, we all know.

Antique Shop

"I'll wrap the Toussaint up for you," he said.
I must have looked alarmed.
I'd just stepped in a moment from the rain.
To try to dodge that lady,
the persistent one,
and failed —
she'd come in after me,
obstructing me amid the objets d'art,
and blocking me among the bric-a-brac.
And yet he'd dealt with her, unasked.
unhurried, but with quiet mastery:
attention, then distraction, then goodbye.
The shop-bell rang behind her as she left.
He went back to his desk without a word;
the kind of tact that draws out purchases.
I browsed a bit to show my gratitude,
and buy myself some time, if nothing else.
It was, I saw now, perfectly set out
and much more tasteful than I'd thought at first.
And quite expensive too. No, cancel that.
the price for everything was just what it should be.
"You've got some good stuff." Compliments are cheap.
And yet I meant it too.
He thanked me. Yes, he tried to do his best.
He'd bought the contents of another shop,
in Bedd … something-or-other, years ago.
I nodded, tried to look the connoisseur,
whose curiosity was satisfied,
and turned to go. He looked up from his work,
swathing the old Toussaint in bubble-wrap.
"I'll bring it round."
This was worse than the attentive lady earlier —
I searched for words. Found none. "A gift," he said.
"Now that we're neighbours."
Were we? Had we ever met before?
I didn't like to ask. I'm new in town.
But in these places I guess word goes round.
"I know the house," he said. I didn't doubt.
I thanked him. He was welcome anytime.

I meant that too.
I thought perhaps of buying something now.
To show goodwill. And then I thought again.
That isn't how it works. That much I know.
You can't repay. Accept the gift and go.

VISITORS

I

Voice

Excuse me, it began. It spoke to me
from somewhere in my head. Excuse me please.
It brought no disrespect with its disease.
You could not fault it for discourtesy.
And yet it came in like it had the right:
a landlord entering a tenant's place,
the absent owner, voice without a face.
Possession can afford to be polite.
And now I am a stranger in my skull,
an eavesdropper afraid what he will find,
sojourner where I had been sovereign.
And only if there comes a moment's lull
do I dare ask: excuse me. Do you mind?
Could I please have my reason back again?

II

Return ticket

It was some six months after he had died
that I saw him at the station, large as life,
with all the weekday travellers passing by.
He looked preoccupied, but self-possessed,
and unsurprised when I approached him there.
Now, I should add, we hadn't parted well.
A difference of opinion, shall we say?
Putting it mildly. But what's done is done.
Least said is soonest mended. If that's true,
then we should have been mended long ago.
But stubborness, and principle, and fear
prevented us. I claim no virtue here.
And now to get a chance to make amends,
was better late than never – literally.
And reappearing from the other side
must surely give permission to approach
despite estrangement, guiltiness or shame.
I touched his arm. I'm not demonstrative,
but the occasion seemed to warrant it.
As did, I must say, curiosity.
He was as solid, though, as you or I.
His overcoat was new. I noticed that.
I said how well he looked. It somehow seemed
congratulations were appropriate.
He had, in fairness, brought off quite a feat,
and, in the greater scheme of life and death,
our differences must be set aside.
But here's the thing: we spoke, that much was true.
But stiff, standoffish, like we were before.
Not quite as bad, perhaps, but not much less.
Death, I was learning, does not separate,
but neither does it simply sanctify.
It was so awkward that I looked around
for something safe that I could comment on.
And when I turned around again, he'd gone.

III

VVIP

That was the day the devil came to call.
We had no notice, almost: just an hour.
Enough to make you nervous, not enough
for second thoughts or making other plans.
And we were curious too – who wouldn't be?
Our CEO came in, preoccupied,
holding a clipboard and a measuring tape,
Apparently, Old Nick likes symmetry.
Who knew? I would have thought that anarchy
was more his style. Still, we all live and learn.
The boardroom table had to be just so;
the chairs all spaced exactly as he said.
No one allowed to touch them. Then he came.
We heard a voice outside: "He's young today!"
Excited. That's what fame and power can do.
And in he came, yes, younger than you thought.
And not well dressed, or not that I could see.
A suit, but not quite fitting. And no smile.
And no eye contact either, just a glance,
not interested at all, just passing through.
He shook our hands, too quickly, and moved on.
I got the handshake wrong. It didn't fit.
And as he went, with all his entourage,
I felt a sense of failure. I still do.

IV

Homecoming

I was not asleep.
Let me make that clear.
Not in some hypnogogic state
before awakening,
a diary page for dream to write upon.
So when the door was shyly opened
and when I felt the pressure on my bed
and when my hand was taken gently
and held a moment
for this first time
by yours,
my daughter,
I knew what only they can know
who welcome back
the one who had to go.

V

Crow

The crow jumped in through the half-open window,
with a strip of paper in his beak
like the scrolled heart of a fortune cookie.
He dropped it on the bedside table,
I could just make out the words.
"Do not believe the Bible,"
or some such dogma.
He jumped back to the window and flew off.
I was preoccupied and left the paper there.
Time enough, I thought, to read it over,
work out what it meant to say, and why.
A short while later, he came back again,
and snatched the strip with what looked like disdain
that I had not yet heeded it, and left,
as I reached out to take it back, and failed.
And though I tried to tempt him to return,
and traced the flight of what I thought was him
from telegraph pole to rooftop and away.
I never will find out what those words say.

VI

Found

The years had simply left no mark on her:
that was the thing that struck me first of all;
more than the shock of seeing her again,
after – what? – thirty years?
She hadn't changed.
There was no explanation.
She was here,
welcome and inconvenient at once.
But more than welcome.
More than anything.
I picked her up and kissed her hair.
My love, I said.
I never say those words.
My love.
I never say those words,
my love.

VII

Emissary

They sent me here to frighten you, she said.
Her blue eyes bright with something close to pride.
Younger than me by some way, pretty too –
which somehow made her challenge all the worse.
I wasn't frightened. Let me make that clear.
Angered, perhaps, at the effrontery,
that she should think those eyes would work on me.
My job was gone. That much was certain now.
And no great loss. I know how to survive.
They sent me here to frighten you. Again.
What C-Suite schemer had despatched her here?
Some maudlin mentor, drunk on anecdote,
who thinks that all men think the same as him.
I gave her back her stare as if to say.
You cannot frighten me. My eyes are grey.

Goodbye to a home.

With no-one else have we spent
so much time, been more
ourselves, cared less
what people say. The world sees
what we want it to, but you
saw what we never showed the working day.

Time's freeholder, you keep
a different measure,
to our mortgaged months.
You have wisdom for us,
should we wish.

The keys have scratched the paint
around the lock that always
let us in. One stair still creaks,
and will, when we move on,
as now – transients that we are – we must.

No heart could be as open as your door
No care could match the shelter that you gave.

And so, this sorrow pays the debt of love,
the last instalment of the loan we owe.
We trust our tenure to your memory,
and bless your hearth,
and those whom you will welcome
when we go.

A new home

I wonder if we could begin this way?
If we could set aside the words we use
habitually for all our habitations.
You know the ones I mean:
buying and selling, cash and equity,
possession, occupation, ownership.
Is all that really necessary? What must
you think of us who think that way?

So, conscious that we are still strangers here,
that this is your place more than it is ours,
whatever papers might say otherwise,
let us acknowledge now your prior claim;
that we can never know this space like you;
you are the indigene, we the immigrants.
We will, each of us, learn each other's ways,
trade sustenance for shelter: give, receive.

For our part, we will honour those you knew
before us. We are worth no more than they.
For yours, we trust that you will not withhold
the welcome you were always made to give.

Whatever time we spend here will be shared,
and all possession is reciprocal;
we will, I hope, discover we belong
one to another as the months go by,
which is more fellowship than ownership,
a better way to share this land, this light.
And let us take our time about it too –
this is what we were made for, we and you.

Rain in Brooklyn

It kept me company all night, the rain;
not for a moment did it slacken off,
drumming the decking, improvising jazz,
riffing its syncopation on the roof,
rapping out rhythms on the balcony.
Nature's all-nighter, with the streets for stage.
Out back, the nameless tree is almost bare,
the leaves so few you rarely see them fall,
just notice they grow scarcer every day.
November takes the brownstones down a shade
and turns the white new-rendered condo grey.
Another jet climbs out of JFK,
grinding through the rainclouds to the sun,
and each departure serves to hold you here,
where every season teaches us to choose
rain where we love, not sunshine far away.

Ossuary,

(St Leonard's Church, Hythe, Kent)

Instead of stained glass, it is filled with skulls,
this Gothic arch, here in the cobwebbed crypt.
Darkness, not daylight, stares through them at you.
The walls are thighbones, stacked like surplus stock,
still serviceable, though their use-by date
expired many centuries ago.
Who knew the English did this kind of thing?
Where is the reticence, the euphemism,
the understatement that can look on death
and say "A dreadful nuisance", "What a bore"?
This is what we expect from Mexicans:
Dia del Muerto, dancing skeletons.
Not here in Hythe. Not in the C of E.
But there they are. And there *we* are, I guess,
sooner or later, stacked or solitary.

Nemo Separabit

We say we take our leave. I don't know why
that verb more than another. Who can say?
But someone, onetime, felt their world grow less
when one who'd shared their table went away.

Obedient to our idioms as we are,
we must, it seems, deprive when we depart:
a bookshelf cleared, belongings put away,
another vacant room within the heart.

Yet what's that line in Two Corinthians?
Grace is sufficient for your weakness, yes?
Paul had his share of partings and of pain,
and found it made him more beloved, not less.

It's what our lives are made of – moving on.
It's time we lack, not love. One thing I know
the measure should not be how long we stay,
but how much grace is needed when we go.

Connection

I ran from you.
But in my white dress.
So that in the dark forest
where I hid myself,
you could find me.

Palimpsest

Clear them away,
the words, the writings,
all the wrong beliefs.
Scratch out the sayings,
tear up the teachings.
Beneath them all
there is still the hard stone
of sacrifice.
There is still the great circle
of my love.

A Marriage

For thirty years she loved him, or she tried,
but what she gave him, without price or pride,
was just a hazel staff cut from a hedge
that at the journey's end is set aside.

Cemetery

I sometimes wonder just what brings me here
to walk these silent gardens of the dead,
not just when autumn rains return each year
or when the oak tree leaves are turning red,
but when this dreamless dormitory is dressed
in spring with silver silk that spiders spin,
and when the sculpted names of those who rest
are warmed by sun more constant than our kin.
Perhaps the certainty. These stone signs set
their limits to our liability.
Perhaps because they show each lifetime's debt
is guaranteed an endless amnesty.
Perhaps because the diamonds of the dew
are not just for the saints, but sinners too.

THE SECRET OF FIRE

The Secret of Fire

A way that we cannot know.
The burning diamonds of the snow.

The green tide time cannot tame.
Each grassblade, a sacred flame.

The heaven we can never hold.
The oak grove is molten gold.

The rosebud's ruby on the briar
each spring is a secret fire.

★★★★★

The burning bush

There is a desert in the heart
as in the wilderness.
Traverse its distance forty days
it never will grow less.

And seek for its circumference
for forty years and more
the loneliness you sought to leave
is nearer than before.

There is no guide to go with you;
no map can mark the way.
The bush can burn for those who leave
and burn for those who stay.

★★★★★

Wildfire

The smallest spark can start a blaze
whose smoke puts out the sun;
a light can darken all your days
until the days are done.

But wildfire opens seeds that never grow
unless it cracks their shell:
the pillared halls of paradise are all
the handiwork of hell.

And wildfire that will make the woods a waste,
will bring the orphaned creature to your door,
will make the wild your neighbour in the night,
while ashes lie like manna on the floor.

★★★★★

Firefly

One time and one time only
did I discern desire;
it wove about me as I walked
a filament of fire.

And came with me for company
as far as I could say,
a spiralling scintilla
to watch me on my way.

And made of me its gravity
as far as I could tell,
a tiny sun that took my soul
as centre – for a spell.

★★★★★

Campfire

Our firelight draws a circle in the dark,
to welcome every wanderer from the cold.
It was not lit to keep the stranger out
and any traveller can share its gold.

So take your seat beside us;
this is no watchman's light.
Beloved and betrayer,
share warmth on a winter's night.

★★★★★

Sacred Fire

You sever us from Eden with a sword,
and lead us through the desert by your light.
You make your prophets' word a burning coal,
and tend the lonely temple lamp at night.

You keep your silence in the desert blaze,
and speak your secret in the lightning storm.
You hide the sun's face like a candle flame,
and send a star to keep a stable warm.

Your love can make the hearts within us burn
and let the firelight reveal our shame.
You call the broken fellowship to feast,
and teach us to forgive in tongues of flame.

Your wisdom is the sunlight and the snow.
Your beauty is the rosebud and the briar.
Teach us to know the shadow and the light,
and fill our hearts today with sacred fire.

Mining Disaster Memorial

We do not ask you to remember us:
you have your lives to live as we had ours,
and ours we spent on life, not memory.
We ask you only this – that you live well,
here, in the places that our labour built,
here, beneath the sky we seldom saw,
here, on the green earth whose black vein we mined,
and feel the freedom that we could not find.

ABERFAN

Commissioned to accompany an exhibition of historic pictures by Life *magazine photographer I.C. 'Chuck' Rapoport for the 50th anniversary of the deaths of 144 people including 116 children, in the Aberfan Disaster of October 21, 1966.*

The graves at Aberfan

The hearts of every woman, every man –
for distance is no hindrance to dismay –
go to the rows of graves at Aberfan.

The prayers of every capel, every llan,
bring to the village where no children play
the hearts of every woman, every man.

Those who can find no God and those who can,
saints who despair and apostates who pray
go to the rows of graves at Aberfan.

The separation that no sense can span
will break forever, one October day,
the hearts of every woman, every man.

You who believe that God must have a plan –
tell it to those whose memories today
go to the rows of graves at Aberfan.

All that we fear the most since fear began,
the tide of black no love can keep at bay.
The hearts of every woman, every man
go to the rows of graves at Aberfan.

★★★★★

48

Hidden

The springs beneath the mountain
have never ceased to flow,
but what they tell the darkness
only the night can know.

★★★★★

★★★★★

Life

(Local miners reading Chuck Rapoport's work in Life *magazine)*

Life is too big,
though children never know –
their world a nature table, miniature,
seeds on a tray, a garden in a jar,
four walls of cut-out prints of autumn leaves
and a calendar that counts to Christmas.

Life is too big.
They never tell you that.
You're never wise enough, never mature.
Take it from me:
your heart is never big enough
to hold it all – the deluge of the dark.
Stars are too distant
and the griefs too great.

Life is too big.
We try to make it fit
our columns and our canvases,
our lenses and our lines,
to make the immeasurable commensurate
with what we can contain:
words on a page,
a garden in a jar.

★★★★★

The journalist

You are not there to weep.
You are there because they are weeping.
And the world must know.

You are not there to show us how you care.
You are there to show how they care.
So the world can care too.

You will not be thanked.
You will not be loved.
Not even by yourself.

The words you did not say,
the tears you did not shed,
will come back to you
years afterwards, when no-one will remember
and no-one understands
that ink can bring enlightenment
but always stains the hand.

★★★★★

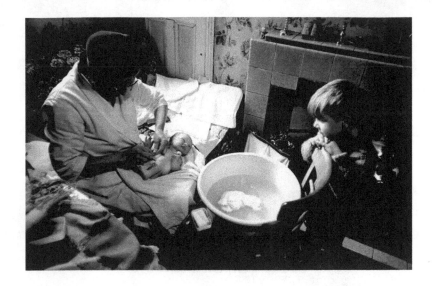

★★★★★

The newborn

(The first baby born since the disaster)

This must be what they mean by hearth and home –
tight as the towelling cloths,
sure as the practised hands.
warm as the fire.

Don't ask from where the coal has come, or how,
simply enjoy the warmth it gives,
for now.

★★★★★

★★★★★

The minister

(The Revd, Kenneth Hayes, who lost his ten-year-old son, Dyfrig. The picture was taken as he preached on the Sunday following the disaster)

'Where was your God?' they asked the preacher man.
He answered: "He was down in Aberfan."
"And what did He do there?" the people said.
"He dug", he answered. "Till His fingers bled."

COVID MASS

The Empty Church

These stones were set by what you cannot see:
by faith and fear,
abstractions now that move no masonry.
Only music now can fill this space,
belief's long-widowed bride,
the slowly-fading shade of certainty.

In the hard acoustic
of agnosticism,
we attune to the eternal's elegy,
epiphenomenon, not epiphany,
attentive still, though in absentia,
as God may be.

★★★★★

Absences

After the play, the ghost light on the stage.
The scent of faith's pressed flower on the page.

A sun-bleached poster for a vanished show.
The yellow grass after the travellers go.

The forest shower when the rain moves on.
The signs still point the way. The place is gone.

But in the night that has no mariner's mark,
a dead star's light is better than the dark.

★★★★★

Questions

The tired trick of teleology
still promises completeness up ahead,
as though you somehow learn the more of life
the closer that it brings you to the dead.

But this is a pilgrimage to poverty,
life leaves you one day poorer every night
and further off from wisdom every day,
and all you learn is that no answers come,
though that might count as wisdom, in a way.

This is the end of searching, when you know
that revelation has no rendezvous,
and, standing in God's presence as they do,
before the only answer they should need,
even the angels have their questions too.

★★★★★

Reckoning

In the end it is the flesh that fails, not you.
Though pain may try to tell you otherwise.
You could have loved more – true.
So could we all.
But you loved as much as you are suffering now.
The books will balance finely:
loss for love,
remorse for your omissions.
You have paid.

★★★★★

Lent

What a letting go this Lent has been.
The appetite is not deferred but dead;
the knife not sharpened to a sheen
but snapped instead.

I am glad of it.

To know I am not needed
is a fugitive's amnesty,
and it feels a lot like absolution
to accept absurdity.
Never to be missed
and not to mind
is a mirror shattered
that always showed too much
and was not kind.
I do not know if this is wrong.
I know it to be true.
I might have called it failure;
it could be freedom too.

★★★★★

Sabbath

There will be a time for them:
a Sunday, perhaps.
No tasks. No visitors.
No calls to make.
It will be neither summer nor autumn,
winter nor spring.
And there will be all the time,
all the time in the world,
to go to them again,
those places that you left unwillingly,
vowing you would return,
time to meet again the ones you loved,
and missed the moment that their story closed.
So many years you want to live again.
So many things that time has put away.
There will be time for them
one Sabbath day.

★★★★★

Redemption

This emptiness has no reproach for you.
What you withheld does not diminish it;
it grows no greater because of what you gave.
The terms it gives are unconditional.
For mercy, any measure is enough,
So set your shortcomings as surety,
and failure as fulfilment
and make the one transaction of your trust:
the debt of living is redeemed with dust.

(*from*) Between the Stormclouds and the Sea

(Romney Marsh, Kent)

Seeking

This is why you came,
because here you can run no further,
because here, you feel, each morning,
the horizon's invitation,
because, each day,
you see the open secret of the sky,
because here you listen each night
to the sea's insistent catechism,
because, if there are no answers,
you know, at least,
you have not hidden from the questions.

★★★★★

The Marsh Churches

You do not need faith to come here.
You do not need to know
before you lift the iron latch
and feel, as you step inside,
the sacred chill.
Believer, unbeliever,
the silence that awaits will be the same
and always will.
The light through the leaded panes,
the same;
the birdsong in the cemetery,
the same.
And this is comfort
should you wish:
that there is nothing you can say or do
can make this place do less than welcome you.
Your faith, your failings …
do you think they care,
the silent saints whose names these churches bear?

(from) *Deus dat Incrementum*
(Marlborough College, Wiltshire)

The Wisdom of the Land.

The summer days we never thought would pass,
are hidden like the chalk beneath the grass,
and what we love the most we keep from sight,
like earth's dark mantle makes the chalk more white.

We may not ever know the reason why
they raised the rich earth up against the sky.
They could not know the future that would be
and yet their labours shaped the land we see.

We have our own time's tasks, and cannot know,
how we may be remembered when we go,
yet in this place we find the strength to stand,
and in the bones, the wisdom of the land.

★★★★★

The Sky Above the Downs

A feeling that you know but cannot name.
Whatever days may come or men may say,
the sky above the downs is still the same.

As wide as when the first wayfarers came
millennia ago, or yesterday.
A feeling that you know but cannot name.

Fortune or failure, sanctity or shame,
sunlight or stormcloud, increase or decay:
the sky above the downs is still the same.

The courage that you trust but never claim;
belief you neither boast of nor betray:
a feeling that you know but cannot name.

The faith as calm as a refiner's flame
when every fear and falsehood falls away:
the sky above the downs is still the same.

The love beyond all blessing and all blame,
when silence is the only way to pray.
A feeling that you know but cannot name;
the sky above the downs is still the same.

Wrth Ddŵr a Thân / By Water and Fire

(For the opening of the Fifth National Assembly)

The stream that knows the stone that set it free
can meet with open heart the open sea.

Heb rwysg na rhemp na rhwystr
yr afon deithia 'mlaen.
Mae'r dŵr sy'n llifo'n dawel
yn tarddu yn y maen.

The sunset makes a pathway through the sea.
The fire that made the chain can make the key.

Ar ddinas neu ddiffeithwch,
yr un goleuni glân.
Os arall ydyw'r aelwyd
yr un yw gwres y tân.

(from) *Adre' Dros 'Dolig* / Home for Christmas

The Saviour in the Shawl

It's the old familiar music for the thousandth time
and the songs are snowflakes whirling round the Word.
In two thousand years the writers have run out of rhyme,
since a baby's cry in Bethlehem was heard.
And all the songs are old ones and the story's still the same.
and there's nothing new that we can say at all.
And every year, the snow comes for a shorter stay
and fewer seek the Saviour in the shawl.

I sometimes wonder why the Dayspring chose the night
to bring salvation to the stable door.
Perhaps because we need it most when there's no light
and the powerful forget about the poor.
And now I find my faith has failed from year to year,
and my heart has lost the hope it used to hold.
But if Christ comes to Creation, then you'll find him here –
when dawn is distant and the night is cold.

But we still sing, because the night's still so lonely.
We still sing, for the poor still feel the pain.
We still sing, for every birth is a beginning,
and hope is in a mother's arms again.

The songs speak more of sorrow than salvation now,
and it hurts my heart to hear 'O Holy Night.'
The lamp of faith burns lower now from hour to hour.
Its flame will never last until the light.
But if this lonely vigil's what we have to keep,
and there's no-one there to hear us when we call,
we'll hold the hand of Heaven and we'll let him sleep
and clasp him all the closer in the shawl.

But we still sing, because the night's still so lonely.
We still sing, for the poor still feel the pain.
We still sing, for every birth is a beginning,
and hope is in a mother's arms again.

A Welsh Prayer

Almighty God,
whose faithfulness is like the mountains
and whose mercy like the rain,
whose wisdom ordained that the lines should fall for us
in delightful places,
grant us a spirit of thanksgiving
and give us strength to serve
that when you call on us
we shall be ready
to answer for this corner of the earth.

A Welsh Blessing

May God who gave this country to our care,
to be a home, to be the gate of heaven,
give you and all those you love
the strength of its hills,
and the peace of its deep places,
to bring you hope in all your coming days.

(from) The Souls of the Righteous

Lux aeterna

And let all those who leave our company,
early or late, together or alone,
find the road they follow is familiar
and find that every turning takes them home.

And let there be a heaven all the higher
for those who had to find their way through hell,
and let there be forgiveness all the greater
for those who broke their faith before they fell.
A mystery all the greater for the answer,
a darkness all the deeper for the star,
a sunlight all the purer for the shadow,
a beauty made more perfect by the scar.

Notes

'One Human Soul'. Shortly after we moved into our new house in Brecon, this sign appeared on a lamppost outside. I tagged it with this poem of response.

'Familiar'. Urdd Gobaith Cymru (The Welsh League of Hope), known as the Urdd, is a youth organisation which promotes activities, including sport, through the medium of Welsh. '*Diwedd Mawr* ' is a mild exclamation.

'Rain in Brooklyn'. With thanks to my good friend Seana Anderson, with whom I was staying while in New York for the premiere of 'The Souls of the Righteous' at Carnegie Hall on the Centenary of the Armistice on November 11 2018.

'Ossuary'. This crypt of this medieval church has the largest collection of human bones in Britain: hundreds of skulls dating back at least 700 years.

'*Nemo Separabit*'. Commissioned for the departure of Rebecca Matthews as Director of Goodenough College, London. The College motto is '*Unitas in Sapientia Nemo Separabit* "Wisdom in Unity No-one Shall Separate'.

'Sacred Fire'. A version of this poem was set to music by Sarah Class and performed by South African soprano Pretty Yende and the Coronation Orchestra for the Coronation of King Charles III in Westminster Abbey on May 6th 2023.

'Mining Disaster Memorial'. Commissioned to accompany a painting by artist Roy Guy in Newbridge Miners' Institute to commemorate the 268 men and boys killed in the Prince of Wales Colliery disaster, Abercarn, on September 11, 1878. The poem was read by actor Michael Sheen in his 2015 programme about the Chartist Rising, *A Valleys Rebellion*. Picture reproduced with the permission of Roy Guy.

'Aberfan'. With the exception of 'The Graves at Aberfan', all the commissioned poems were originally in Welsh, and appear here in translation. Pictures are reproduced with the permission of I.C. "Chuck" Rapoport, who was one of the first photographers on the scene in the aftermath of the tragedy. The project was a joint commission with the poet Tony Curtis, who wrote a separate suite of original English poems. As a young newspaper reporter for the *Merthyr Express*, I was responsible for the paper's coverage of the 20th anniversary of the disaster in 1986 and knew many of the parents, including Kenneth Hayes. Thirty years later, I was involved in the 50th anniversary commemorations.

'Covid Mass'. Commissioned by the JAM on the Marsh festival, Romney Marsh, Kent, to accompany a performance of Faure's *Requiem* in St Leonard's Church, Hythe, to commemorate the lives lost in the Covid pandemic. Also published in *Arrival at Elsewhere*, an anthology of Covid writing curated by Carl Griffin (Against the Grain, 2020).

'Between the Stormclouds and the Sea'. Commissioned by the JAM on the Marsh festival, in 2021 with the composer Jack Oades.

'*Deus dat Incrementum*'. Commissioned by Marlborough College, Wiltshire, with the composer Paul Mealor, to mark the College's 200th anniversary in 2022, The College's Latin motto *Deus dat Incrementum* means 'God will give the increase'. The grounds of the college include a 4,000-year-old burial mound associated with the legend of Merlin. The town of Marlborough's motto is '*Ubi nunc sapientis ossa Merlini*' 'Where now are the bones of wise Merlin?'

'*Wrth Ddŵr a Thân*'. Commissioned by the National Assembly for Wales, now the Senedd / Welsh Parliament, to music by Paul Mealor for the official opening of the Fifth Assembly in June 2016. The Pierhead Building, part of the Senedd estate, has a mural with the words '*Wrth Ddŵr a Thân*', ('By Water and Fire') a reference to the coal, steel and maritime industries. The Welsh verses here convey the sense that the river, which takes its way so calmly, has its source in the rock, that the same light illuminates city and wasteland, and that though hearths may differ, the warmth of the fire is the same.

'The Saviour in the Shawl'. Translated from the Welsh original. Commissioned by University of Wales Trinity St David as part of the musical '*Adre' Dros 'Dolig* / Home for Christmas' with the composer Eilir Owen Griffiths. Later also set to music by Sarah Class and released as a single.

'A Welsh Prayer'. Commissioned in 2013 for the North Wales International Music Festival to mark the 65th birthday of HRH The Prince of Wales, with music by Paul Mealor, and later performed at the memorial service for H.M. The Queen in Llandaff Cathedral on September 16 2022. The reference is to Psalm 16, verse 6, which in the Church in Wales lectionary is set for St David's Day: "The lines are fallen unto me in pleasant places; yea, I have a goodly heritage." The reference to 'strength to serve' is drawn from The Prince of Wales's German motto, '*Ich Dien*', 'I serve.' The final line refers to the legend, given in Giraldus Cambrensis's late 12th Century account, *A Journey Through Wales* in which an old man at Pencader in west Wales is questioned by the English King Henry II in 1162 about the future of his nation and replies by saying: "I do not think that on the Day of Judgement any nation other than that of the Welsh, or any other language, will give answer to the Supreme Judge for this corner of the earth." A Welsh Blessing is a companion piece, commissioned a decade later for Paul Mealor and the North Wales International Music Festival in September 2023 to mark The King's 75th birthday. The references are to Genesis 28: 17, and Psalm 95.

'*from* The Souls of the Righteous; *Lux Aeterna*'. Commissioned in 2018 by the Chapel Royal of Scotland to mark the Centenary of the Armistice, for music by Paul Mealor, and premiered in Carnegie Hall, New York, and St Mary's Cathedral, Edinburgh.

Thanks and Acknowledgements

My thanks to all at Seren who have made this volume possible: to my patient, supportive and insightful editors Zoë Brigley and Rhian Edwards, and also to Sarah Johnson, Simon Hicks, and, at an earlier stage, Amy Wack.

In addition to those cited in the endnotes, two of the pieces have appeared in print before: 'The Mission' in *Tokens for the Foundlings,* ed. Tony Curtis (Seren, 2012) and 'Caller' in *Where the Birds Sing Our Names,* ed. Tony Curtis, (Seren, 2021). The Aberfan sequence also appeared as a pamphlet in 2016, and the song lyrics have appeared in concert programmes.

As acknowledged in the endnotes, many of the pieces in this volume were commissioned for musical compositions or, in some cases, for visual arts collaborations. I am grateful to all the many composers, festivals and organisations who commissioned the pieces, and to the audiences across the world who have helped shape the work.

As ever, my most heartfelt gratitude and love go to my wife Sally, and our daughters Haf and Alaw.

Also by the author

Non-Fiction

Real Cambridge (Seren, 2021)
The Dragon and the Crescent: Wales and Islam (Seren, 2011)
Real Wrexham (Seren, 2007) Reprinted 2009
The Chosen People: Wales and the Jews (Seren, 2002)
Sefyll yn y Bwlch (University of Wales Press, 1999)

Fiction

Everything Must Change (Seren, 2007)
Rhaid i Bopeth Newid (Gomer, 2004)

Poetry

Lightning Beneath the Sea (Seren, 2012)
Alcemi Dŵr / The Alchemy of Water (Gomer, 2013),
with Tony Curtis
Achos (Barddas, 2005)
Ffiniau / Borders (Gomer, 2002) with Elin ap Hywel
Cadwyni Rhyddid (Barddas, 2001). Reprinted 2002
Adennill Tir (Barddas, 1997)

Anthologies

The Big Book of Cardiff Eds. Peter Finch & Grahame Davies
(Seren, 2005)
Gŵyl y Blaidd / Festival of the Wolf, Eds. Tom Cheesman,
Grahame Davies and Sylvie Hoffmann
(Parthian/Hafan, 2006)
Nel pais de la borrina (WFP Editorial, 2004)
No pais da bretama (VTP Editorial, 2004)
Oxygen, Eds. Amy Wack & Grahame Davies (Seren, 2000)

Printed in the USA
CPSIA information can be obtained
at www.ICGtesting.com
LVHW040234061024
792941LV00007B/201